Epic Philosophies in Love, War, &
Reasoning Vol. 3:

Where My Heart Beats

By
Thomas S. Doland

Dedicated to my mother, Ida.

TABLE OF CONTENTS

Preface

Traveling the world's nations and cultures breaks the mold of encapsulated thinking. It opens human suffering and passion. Societies torn by culture wars worldwide. Reveal the tenderness of the human drama. From towers of power dynasties to hidden slave camps, the orphans of compassion seek asylum.

Mysteries of culture hidden by colorful tradition hide the trauma of caste systems. Heartless governments uprooting families into endless migration to nowhere. Highways of broken dreams and lives seeking hope for new life and fulfillment. These works capture the essence of the ocean's tides and waves of love, desire, passion, and vision.

Let your imagination relocate you to another world. Perhaps the refueling of your own existence. Welcome to the travels into your heart and soul.

Introduction

Journeys of love are like the rising and falling tides. Gentle and embracing. Other times, like the waves crashing and wind-blown. However, it is experienced. It is a necessary component for our emotional well-being. So into the journey of being in love and being out of love, the lyrics and ballads and epic events of this ever-so-changing tell many of our own stories. Let them take you away to tears and fears. Take you into misunderstanding and longing for past relationships to be restored and recovered. At any rate, jump into the flowing streams of emotions in this volume. All about love, romance, and another chance. Enjoy. Let them take you away.

Garden Gate

Through the vine-covered garden gate
While working on the walls
I see you walking along the stone path
Stopping to smell the flowers along the way
Stepping from under the shadowing trees
The sun lights your path

A morning breeze blows
Stirring the fresh morning air
Sunlight glistens on the dew-laden grass
And sparkles rainbow colors like diamonds
I work on the garden walls every now and again

You call me over
To share greetings through the gate
I sometimes only get a glimpse of you
And my heart is stolen away

It's raining today
So I know I won't see you
Tomorrow may be a chance
The garden is silent the flowers alone
The wall is solemn
I feel it even in my heart

The sun rises on another day
A soft breeze stirs the morning air
The flowers sway as it blows
Across the garden
Will my prayer be answered today

Looking For Love

How can it be you feel so forsaken
How can it be a heart broken apart
How can it be your life so shaken
How can it be true love is so short
Just for a moment passion appears
Just for a moment the heart is made strong
Just for a moment you fight back the fears
Just for a moment this can't be wrong
All in a lifetime
The heart searches deeply
All in a lifetime looking for true love
All in a lifetime looking for meaning
All that it takes is one glance up above
This time it's true
Your heart feels it's right
This time it's true
Another song in the night
This time it's true
The morning will tell
This time it's true
Another heartbreak to tell
Over and over the search will go on
Over and over you'll be left alone
Over and over you'll cry in the night
Over and over you'll be left
Short of sight
Once in a lifetime the heart will cry out
Once in a lifetime true love comes in

Once in a lifetime you will have no doubt
Once in a lifetime you find a true friend
No looking for love on a busy street
No looking for love finding only defeat
No looking for love leaving the heart open bare
No looking for love only heartbreak to share
What's the end of the story
What's left to be told
What's the end of your story
No curtain unfolds
What's the end of the story
God does have a plan
What's the end of the story
You must
Take a stand
True love isn't hasty
True love makes no demands
True love has no compromise
True love never dies

Angel

I have a friend that's an angel
From heaven or earth
Only God can tell
I have a friend that's an angel
I know I'm not mistaken
My heart is really shaken
I have a friend that's an angel
Princess or queen
I know she's special to me
I have a friend that's an angel
Eyes so bright
That they light up the sky
I know it's really real
How true friendship
Makes you feel
I have a friend that's an angel
I'm in love with an angel

You Well Know

I love you
Do you love me
It is not hard to let it show

Will you love me
I love you
It is so hard to let you go

I will show you
Will you show me
Love was alive you well know

I love you
I keep rehearsing
Only the mirror seems to know

Lace and Red Roses

I would give you the sky
If I could find its ends
I would give you a rainbow
From end to end
I would give you the clouds
If they wouldn't slip away
I would find you the pots of gold
If the rain would stay
I would give you the wind
If I could catch it in the leaves
I would give you the stars
If you would be pleased

I would give you bows and ribbons
For your beautiful hair
I would give you lovely flowers
The butterflies share
But all I have are words
To say with my heart
A princess life I wish you
Lace and red roses scented fair
A white carriage
With black steeds reigning
A princess life
In a princes care

Princess

God blessed the earth
With the robe of the sun
He blessed the grass
With the kiss of dew
He blessed the wind
With perfume of flowers scent
He blessed my life
With you

He blessed the mountains
With the crown of snow
He blessed the leaves
In ordaining wind
He blessed the forest
With the sound of the brook
He blessed me with you
As my friend

He blessed the twilight
With the morning star
He blessed the river
With the streams
He blessed the gardens
With refreshing rain

He blessed me
To meet a princess
Of dreams

It's Only About Eight

Called you on the phone
It was only about eight
You answered really rude
Why are you calling so late
I just wanted to hear your voice
You thought I wanted to fall in love

Saw you next day on the street
Tried my best to be nice
You answered really rude
Why do you keep going on
I just wanted to hear your voice
You thought I wanted to fall in love

Maybe I really want to
Is that all so strange

Incurable Romantic

Candle light at the dinner table
Sweet perfume and incense of sable
A quiet evening with a glass of wine
A special place for hearts to dine
It's not a place of getting frantic
It's just the dream
Of an incurable romantic
A night drive down a moonlit road
A fireplace burning on a night so cold
Sharing of heart dreams and plans
It's not a review full of semantics
It's just the heart
Of an incurable romantic
Snuggled on the sofa
Watching a Cinderella story
Sharing an evening
Everything perfect and cozy
One secure with the other
With no plans or antics
It's just the idea
Of an incurable romantic

Beneath The Stars

I hadn't planned this
It wasn't in a book I read
Maybe in a song or two
The tears are here to stay

You walked away
and didn't even look back
I remember we fell in love
How can you forget
We melted in each other's arms
And could not let go

Beneath the stars
Now here we go
Falling apart
Beneath the stars

I whispered your name
But you shook your head
As you walked away
I held my head high
But the tears
Are here to stay

In and Out of Love

In and out of love
You're breaking all the rules
In and out of love
You took me for the fool
I gave you all my love
And now you're leaving
I gave you all my love
It was all so deceiving
In and out of love
You took me by surprise
In and out of love
Now I know your lies
In and out of love
You took my heart away
In and out of love
I wish
That you would stay

You Were Mine

Are there enough laws
To bring you back home
You wandered far away
I remember the night you decided
You pushed common sense away
Now you only draw blanks
No place to go
No place to stay
No place in your heart
For my voice anyway
Remember times we talked
You were mine
We were close
Now you're on your own
You decided to wander away

No Escape

Why am I still writing this letter
I hoped the words
Would stop
They are always the same
I keep throwing away the pages
Yet I start all over again
It always starts with I love you
It always ends the same
It really seems all so simple
Can we start all over again

Another Sunday Morning

It's another Sunday morning
Still have buzzing in my head
Got to get another drink
Can't get out of my bed

It's another Sunday morning
Looked to see that you were gone
Doesn't seem so very strange now
Can't get used to being alone

It's another Sunday morning
Can't get you off my mind
Can't get used to losing you
Should have been more kind

It's another Sunday morning
Still have buzzing in my head
Got to get another drink
Can't get drinkin' off my mind

Never Imagined

Never imagined
My day would take this turn
Never imagined
My heart could break this way
Never imagined
I could love so deeply
Never imagined she would go away

It was all so very innocent
A friendship all unplanned
Our hearts were knit together
As one we went our separate ways

It was all so very innocent
A friendship all unplanned
She told me that it was over
This friendship could not be
In shambles I wept on my knees

That place inside is now vacant
At times my eyes just stare
For a short time there was sunshine
Now those windows are filled with rain

For A Moment

Pictures and thoughts
Of what has been
They have no roots to stay
To keep them in place
Rolling in streams and rivers
Contained by no human way
Time with no beginning
Time with no end
Images in rippling water
Only for moment
Then they slip away

It's better this way
Time is just a moment away
No reflection No picture
Can keep it in its place
Its formed in the mind
Reaching to touch it
And it slips away

Its compelling memories
Ripples in time
Carry them just out of reach
Reflections in the water
Reach to touch it
It disappears
Time in my hands
Grasping to hold it in place
The past vanishes in a moment
Time slips away

Remember

It was late September
As close as I can remember
Our love was a flickering ember
Something deep was lost
But the ring on my finger

It was late November
As close as I can remember
Our love was cold
No reason to linger
But
For the ring on my finger

It was late in December
As close as I remember
The song was gone
Burned in the embers
Gone is the ring
On my finger

It was September
You lost your smile
It was November
For a little while
It was December
Don't you remember

Another Time Another Place

Don't I know you from somewhere
I've seen that heart before
I see the way it thinks and feels
I know I know you I'm sure
You say some things the way I do
I feel we're someway one
Just little comments that you make
That's me all over again
Is there enough magic in moonlight
Does fate have the power to decide
When lives cross such as ours have
I believe God was behind it all
Believe it's the power of destiny
To turn the tide at hand
It's all too amazing to think
Mere humans are in command
One thing I know
I believe in you
To see your heart in flight
Hearing your laughter
Fill the air
Your soul filled with delight
Don't I know you from somewhere
I know you from another place
It must be from sometime before
I can't escape your face
I've seen you flying free
Far above the land

No ropes to tie or bind you
Free from Earth's demands
I saw you riding bareback
A glistening chestnut mare
I've seen myself in that same place
Of that I'm much aware
It would take too many yesterdays
To change decisions made
Tomorrow's decisions are yet to be
A future of plans unmade
All that is within me
Feel our paths ever near
It's almost like I'm with you
Your image always so clear
I feel love come into view
Through all time and space
Our destiny
We will not see
Till our hearts meet
Once again

Never Imagined Revisited

Never imagined it would turn out this way
Never conceived there would be such pain
If love could cover this blunder
I would return to the land of the sane

Never imagined
Things could get so twisted out of shape
It will take years of rearranging
There are things so deeply at stake

Never imagined I would be so old
Before my senses recovered hope
Years flew by in a blur of tears
Before my eyes could see the sun

I know now it was so foolish
To let things go so far
But a heart restrained from love
Had tasted a friendship so deep

The past got swept away in laughter
Never conceived I could feel so free
Something deeper
Than I could ever believe

But forever was not to be

Never conceived I would hear goodbye
Never entered my mind
The thoughts of us happy
Alone again was the last thing
I had in line

All the good intentions
Did not play out so well
We both belonged to others
We both knew all too well

Ending like a sinking ship
Broken wreckage washed ashore
Rearranging pieces of twisted dreams
Still staring into what if

That was never to be

After All

I see I am blind
Thought you would be kind
Thought I would see in your eyes
To see I am blind
I will go back tonight
When there is some light
Still not clear
Too many tears
After all the years
After all
Time heals all blindness
But mine

Tell me true

Summer rain return again
Summer rain
I feel it in the wind
Relief from draught
A hot wind blows
Summer rain comes
Summer rain goes
Summer winds blow
Across the plains

Summer winds search
For summer rains
Relief from a dry place
Draught has set in
Summer rains
Returning again
The heart is dry place
Without summer rain

The search goes on
Love found and
Lost again
A desert heart
Who can sustain
Summer rain
Come once again
Tell me true
Who loves you more

Different Eyes

Here go the memories
Falling from my eyes
Here go the heartaches
Falling from my sky
Nothing seems to stop them
Clouds filled with panorama
Of your face
The natural meeting of two rivers
Now all that is left is a stream of tears
The only thing that is left to trace
If only I had yesterday
I could see with different eyes
Now only a fog of memories
Heartache falling from my sky

Hard Price

You said you would never leave me
You said you would never go away
Now I'm feeling so lonely
There's a price I wouldn't pay
Yes, I made a hasty decision
Made a retreat from respect
Nothing left to hold onto
Can't go on without you
Didn't mean to offend you
Didn't mean to break your heart
I took the hard line
Only considered myself
Didn't think
About your heart
Hard times
Heart break
Bad times
Heart ache
Better to be tender
Better to be kind
Now
There's a hard price
A hard time to pay

Don't Go Away

I wondered out
On the seas and oceans
Left the land
Of wisdom and devotion

If I ask to be forgiven
Can I claim to be a wise man
Will the way to see return
I stopped your love
Just to have my say

I know I erred
In my way
Don't go away
What is a king
Without his queen and castle
What is a queen
Without her king and throne

All I ask
Is to hear you say my name
I'm nothing out here
On my own

I weep
Until no tears are left me
Can't see your face
The ocean mists remain

Can it be I hear you calling
Don't go away

Yesterday

Always going back in time
Reminiscing days gone by
Remembering all the good times
And bad
My how time does fly

There was not a care to be had
It all seemed to just fall in place
There was no weight of responsibility
There was no having to struggle or race

But now reality is here
It's evident time has shown
The whole story was not revealed
How you have to have changed
To have grown

It's okay to think about it
Now and then
Recalling those flighty days
But this is now
And that was then
It commands
A completely new stage

Remembering friends and faces
Those times of frolic and play
But there were lessons learned
To hold on to
Now it's living a whole new way

Buddies you hung with
Places you went
You go back and say
"Remember when"
But time goes on, life goes by
This is now that was then

Hanging on to yesterday's memories
Living on things in the past
Life must go on, changes must come
It's a play with a changing cast

You have to let go to go on
You have to release to proceed
The past has a way of
Holding up life
Not good to keep planting old seed

Let go of the past and its fancies
Let go of the past and its woes
Reach out and obtain your future
Your destiny is waiting
In the folds

Hide Your Heart Away

Looking for other words
When you can't say what you mean
Can't express true feelings
All you can really do is dream
Went a step too far in feeling compassion
What began as caring words
Emotions took over in full fashion
Should have known better
Than to give your heart away

Had it locked up for so long
It yearned for light of day
Somehow someway
Somewhere someday
You'll find a way
To just be a friend
Somehow someway
Somewhere someday
You'll learn
How not to hide your heart away
Should have known
Not to hide it away so long

Just to have someone to care
Makes a decision ever so strong
To just be friends
Someone to share
To dare to not hide your heart away

Thinking you went a mile too far
Your feelings got in the way
What began as innocent caring
Took your heart up in wings
And flew away
Should know better
Than to give your heart away
Had it locked up for so long
It yearned for warmth of day

Somehow someway
Somewhere someday
You'll learn
To just be a friend
Somehow someway
Somewhere someday
You'll learn
How not to hide your heart away
Somehow someway
Somewhere someday

Played The Fool

Old romance came my way
Old romance back into play
Familiar eyes Familiar smile
Familiar memory Familiar style
Elevated heartbeat gave me away
Familiar style comes into play
Eyes give away unspoken desire
Old romance back into play
Games are no place
For the wise to play
Cellphone rings
Expressions show questions
To save the day
Don't need a player
Fooled just a smile away
Stayed to long already
My head cried foul
Best to smile and walk away
She smiled and turned
My heart screamed no
But I played the fool before
Palms sweating as I closed the door

I Think I Will Pass

Wait a minute
I'm supposed to cry about now
If I remember right
You did this before
But I got it down now
It comes as no surprise
I'm supposed to cry now
But I think I will pass
You moved on
So have I
Don't look at me
Like you still care
Don't think I will take you back
Got better things to do
You think I should cry now
It's all about you
Have a great day
But I think I will pass

Freight Trains

Freight trains always sound the same
Seems somehow they call my name
I've no gypsy blood but I feel inside
To break the chains and feel the countryside
Almost feels
Like there is someone in a distant place
Who is calling me but I can't see her face
It always seems to come to a decision
To go away or be held in this derision
Deep inside there is a passion to go
The wheels on the tracks keep calling me on
These crossroads seem to keep coming my way
Keeping their hold on my soul every day
To stay and wrestle with all of life's obstacles
Or follow these rails to the mountains and coasts
I hear that freight train's distant call
Seems now I can't hear anything else at all
Suppose it's time to pack a bedroll and go
A slicker, five dollars, and a peaceful soul
To some it's the wind, the ocean or mountain range
But freight trains always sound the same
The rumble and whistle somehow call my name

Louisiana Bound

I'm following these road signs
Back to Louisiana
It's memories always on my mind
This long lonesome highway
Is about to come to an end
I'll be crossing the ole Mississippi
Just around the bend
I have been following
These road signs back
From where I came
The bayous and the mossy oaks
I've been really missing so
Going down this Louisiana bound road
Back home
Had lost my way
In someone else's dreams
Found this highway in the dark
Now all is right it seems
Now I found this highway
To the treasure in my heart

Bayou Dreams

Found myself in Atlanta Georgia
Lookin' for that pot of gold
Found bright lights and mean streets
Waitin' to buy my soul

Headin' back to Louisiana
Goin' back where I was born
Tired of chasin' empty promises
Back to the fields and poppa's farm

The lights were bright on the horizon
The glow stirred up my mind
I'm headin' back to bayou country
To find a life a little more kind

Goin' to find a big shady oak tree
Lay on back in the lazy breeze
Goin' back to the bayou country
Back to the farm and bayou streams

Ain't goin' back to Atlanta Georgia
Still ain't found that pot of gold
Ain't found no good on mean street
And I ain't goin' to sell my soul

Gonna find some shady oak tree
Lots of moss hangin' in the breeze
Goin' back to bayou country
Back to the farm and bayou dreams

Leaving New York City

Listening to country music on the radio
Playing a song Darlin' Don't You Know
New York had me by the throat
I said that's over today

New York ain't a place
For a country boy to be
Got my truck all loaded up
Won't be stopping' in Tennessee

Texas is the mother of country music
It's the father of wailin' blues
That's why I'm leavin' New York City
Got my boots and walkin' shoes

I said that's it I'm done
Leaving New York today
Won't stop in Nashville, Little Rock
Or New Orleans
Going to the heart of country music
In Texas I'll find my dream
Good bye New York
I'm leaven' now
Got Texas on my mind
Got country music in my soul

Left New York

Where heartbreak
Meets the rain
Left New York
For the Louisiana plains
Things didn't go
As I had planned
Where does heartbreak
Lead to again
In Louisiana
On my front porch
In my rocker
My tear stained shirt
Is in the washer
The sky is clear
So are my eyes
Had someone trusted
Tell me lies
That is one thing
I despise
Back working the fields
On my daddy's tractor
Back in Louisiana
Sugar cane country
That's what my soul
Was truly after

Opelousas Home

Just a lonesome cowboy on the Opelousas Plains
Left the house early again
Sun's breakin' through the clouds
Been a long mornin' in the rain

It's been a lonely place since momma's been gone
I tried to leave a while back
Just to escape the pain
But I'd rather be in this saddle
Drivin' these cattle in this Opelousas rain

I can still see her cookin'
Breakfast at the stove
The chickens in the yard
Waitin' for her impatiently
They been lonely since she's been gone
Nothin's the same

Got her grave next to daddy's
In the graveyard down the road
Passin' by it again this morning'
Lord I miss her so

It's been a lonely farm
Since she's been gone
Ain't never gonna leave
Got no place else I want to go

Cicero's all wet and muddy
Workin' with me on these cows
He's a faithful collie dog
Been around since I was a kid
Always pantin' and waggin' his tail

At the kitchen door waitin' for momma
To toss him a scrap
He don't smile much anymore
He's been a lonely dog since she's been gone

Her apron still layin'
over the back of the chair
At the kitchen table
Her boots she wore in the yard
Still at the door

She'd look up from her cookin' with
Her gentle eyes and smile
Dinner 'bout ready
Get washed up
and take that hat off in the house
Lord I miss her so

Been a real lonely farmhouse
Since she's been gone
But I'll never leave
My Opelousas home

Grand Chenier Cattle Driv'n

Maw maw's brewin' up the coffee
Biscuits in the oven a bakin'
I can smell'm right out in the yard
Between them and the eggs and bacon
Can't say which I love the most

Skeeters ain't bad this mornin'
For the Chenier Ridge that's pretty rare

Sun's up over the oaks already
I'm hearin' cattle comin' down the road
Can't rightly see'm yet
Got a good ground fog set in

Uncle David and the boys are
Drivin' a herd east to Pecan Island
They always stop in for coffee
On the way

While their tyin' up the horses on the fence posts
Cars are makin' their way through the herd
Cattle fillin' up the road ditch to ditch
Far as I can see

Uncle David and the boys always got a chew
Of bull durham
A little drip always at the corner of their mouth
They can roll a cigarette with one hand

Spurs janglin' on the kitchen floor
Gets noisy as everybody is talkin' at one time
Fresh coffee's poured
And everybody's still talkin' at once

Paw Paw and Uncle David move outside
And lean on the gate at the road
Coffee and cigarette in hand

Fog's a liftin' an the cattle are gettin' restless
All the cowboys move outside and mount up
With fresh smokes and a chew
Thanks for the coffee and a wave
See ya'll later

Memories

It's an early August morning
Five o'clock must be
Grandma's big kitchen fan
Pulled in a cool pleasant breeze

The Crescent City morning
Is embraced by her canary's song
The corner bakery is about to open
The stirring isn't far along

Fresh bread and jelly donuts scent
Fill the morning air
The house is filled with activity
Who'll be the first to get there

Every visit to the River Walk
My mind drifts to old Algiers
Across the river to the old steepled church
To Grandma's house and its tall front stairs

Grandma really loved her flowers
They were hanging every place
Her small back yard was planted up
Until there was no more space

I can still hear her sweet old voice
And the yipping of her little dog
I looked forward to every visit
My heart keeps it in a special log

The afternoons were hot and stuffy
As we played on the old front stairs
But a special trip to the corner store
To get popcorn and cold bargs root beer

I can still remember as evening came
The walk around the corner to the park
By the old steepled church with the black ironwork
And the ballgame starting at dark

There was much anticipation
To get to the concession stand
There was no better snow cone around
The memory of it all is still very grand

Something in the atmosphere
Still draws me to this place
Colorful houses on Alix Street
Algiers Point peaceful grace

Louisiana Goldrush

Deckhands move in the dark
Across the damp boat docks at the crowded
Delcambre pier
Shrimpboats'
Cabin and running lights flicker on and
Glow in the dark waters of Bayou Carlin
Marking the hazy figures in the early
Morning fog
Diesel engines come to life
Ice is hurriedly stored for the catch
Of the day
Lines cast off
Nets and rigging secured
Captain Jimmie, coffee in hand
Works the Connie Ann slowly
In the dawns darkness
Gliding quietly as a ghost
Down the sleepy bayou stream
Dawn stillness stirred
Lights eerily shimmer across the wake
Masts strung with ropes like a web
Nets suspended wings seine the wind
Ready to harvest the riches
Of Vermillions vast bay
Purple Martins in acrobatic flight
Chase a mornings feast
Shrill cries of the gulls
Break the mourning drone of the diesels

Dawns sun flourishes
Its light breaks the horizon
Casting brilliant rays across the bay
Salt spray fills the air as
The bow breaks through the waves
Dolphins accompany the sleek craft
Anticipating a harvest of their own
Gulls sweep down to the orchestra
Of the bay
Nets are lowered into the dark waters
The vessel slows and follows
The feeding gulls
Bacon and egg sandwiches are carefully
Unwrapped for breakfast
The crew busily prepares for work
The diesels groan from the
Weight of the catch
The nets are pulled in
Clearing the water
Another seafood harvest
Of Vermillion Gold

Timeless

Captured in the framework
Of a timeless place
A wooded garden of moss laden oaks
Sprawl over the lazy bayou's
Secret Stillness
The sun filtered in the misty haze
Stirs the egrets nesting place
And reflects into the wooded cover

Smoke drifts lazily from a cottage chimney
An aged abode nestled neatly
Away in the wooded scape
In a peace undisturbed

Dew drops wash the leaf carpeted ground
The barking of a squirrel
And the fussing of a jay in the palmetto
Announce the dawns breaking

An aged drawn figure
Descends on the creaking
Wooden steps
In straw hat and coveralls
Traps and cane pole in hand
He descends to the pirogue
Tied up by a cypress on the bank

Pushing off onto lily pad covered
Shallows
He disappears to the bayou's
Secret storehouse
Age in the ageless
Time in the timeless
Captured on the canvas
A timeless place
Louisiana
Lost Bayou

Texas Outlaw Country Music

Texas ain't just another place
It's where I call my home
My roots run deep in Texas
Playing outlaw country music
All day long

Texas ain't just another place
It's where I met my wife
My kids have roots in Texas
Outlaw country music
is my life

Texas ain't just another place
The band likes hanging and
Playing music at my house
My wife likes to cook for everyone
She's the best woman around

Texas ain't just another place
It's where I call my home
My roots run deep in Texas
Playing outlaw country music
All day long

Texas Ten Miles

Getting out of Arizona
Tired of the sun
And blowing sand
Driving on back to Texas
Through lightening
And the pouring rain

Headin' straight to Austin
Ghost clouds blowing in the skies
Getting' out of Arizona
Get the blowin' sand out of my eyes

Loaded my old guitar and dog
Gonna find a country band with luck
Texas sign ten miles ahead
Outlaw country music playin' in my head

Pulled up outside of Austin
What an awesome sight to see
Country music on the radio
My truck my dog my guitar and me

In my old truck
With my guitar and dog
To the Texas music scene
Country music born and bred
Home of outlaw country music
That's where I'll lay my head

Radio playing outlaw country music
Austin Texas straight ahead
Got myself out of Arizona
In Texas I make my bed

Abilene Girl

I've been riding long
Been riding hard
In this blazing Texas sun
Been pushing steers to Kansas City
Gettin' my money
And I'm on the run

Got a girl back in Abilene
I been longin' hard to see
She was wavin' bye last time
I saw her
I know she's waitin' there for me

Ain't no blazin' sun in Texas
Ain't no lightnin' in the sky
Ain't no trail ride to Kansas City
Keep me from my Abilene bride
Yippie Yi Yay
Yippie Yi Yo

Headed back to the Texas plains
Yes I know
Yippie Yi Yay
Yippie Yi Yo
Got a girl waitin' there for me
Yes I know

I've been ridin' hard
Been ridin' long
On this trail ride to her heart
When I get this ring on her finger
We will never be apart

Got a girl back in Abilene
Her hair's bright as the sun
Got green eyes like Texas plains
In her heart I'm the only one

Texas

Remember the cowboy stories
The images recalled so clear
Cattle drives on the Texas plains
Huge herds of longhorn steers

Raising dust that could reach the clouds
Long days in the driving rain
Sunsets that set the sky on fire
Moonlit nights on the mountain range

Chuck wagons laid out for an evening meal
Campfires glowing in the night
Saddles and bedrolls laid out on the ground
Guitars and harmonicas fill the silence

Sentries ride the midnight watch
Coyotes howling all about
Tales and stories told around the fire
Lightning fills the Texas sky

About the Author

Author Thomas S. Doland served in the military as an infantryman from 1969 to 1975. During this stint, he learned something of the art of war. He was married in 1969 and had two daughters: one in 1974 and one in 1976. He had a deep experience with God in 1976, which captured his life for missionary service to Africa, India, South America, and Mexico. His love for humanity grew and continues to be his reason to live and breathe. He is directing and financing a school for child slaves in a brickyard in Pakistan, keeping him focused on presenting his writings to challenge and provoke thought outside of common life. Love embraces him, and he hopes for love to embrace you to seek and fulfill your purpose.

www.ingramcontent.com/pod-product-compliance
Lightning Source LLC
Chambersburg PA
CBHW052359060726
47592CB00019B/1641